Hustle Like an Immigrant

5 Qualities of Successful People

Saikou Camara

Contents

Dedication

Falling and failing are guarantees life offers us. We will all get our turn. The wisdom is not just in getting back up, it is in helping other people do the same when they fall because you know how it feels to be down.

This book is dedicated to all the people dealing with insecurities. The truth is we all have them, whether we admit it or not. I want you to know that it is okay. You don't have to be perfect or live a perfect life, you only need to live a purposeful life and strive for excellence. While perfection is elusive, excellence is attainable. You are not created to be perfect, but you are created to serve a purpose.

To all the people dealing with character assassination, falsehood against your person, and fake news, listen! Some of you are doers, but the enemies are slanderous and character assassins. Because they cannot produce results, they slander to distract you from producing. If their cynicism and negative depiction of you doesn't fit you, they will try to make you fit their description of you. It is a form of profiling. Don't look at what has been said about you. Look in the mirror, that's who you are today. Look onto your imaginations, that's who you are aspiring to become.

I'm writing these words at the risk of sounding or coming off confrontational or evangelical. That's not my intent. The sole purpose is to help someone who is going through *it* to get through *it*. I'm here to say I feel your pain, and the good Lord got you.

The human soul is three dimensional: your heart or will, your mind or thoughts, and your emotions or feelings. God rules the world through man, the devils also seek control of the world through man's soul. Every day you wake up, you are serving as a living vessel for either God or the devil. What you feed your soul with will determine who takes control over you. Every time you set out to do something good, know that you are subsequently wagering a challenge against the devil. It becomes a struggle between your will and that of the devil. You against the devil on your own, you will lose all the time. You need spiritual guidance to get you through. You must anchor your faith in something bigger than both you and the devil.

You must understand some things - some of you are losing your battles because you are fighting behind enemy lines, in the devil's territory, it's natural habitat. The devil does not fight fair, it bears false witness, it spreads falsehood, and it duels in gossip and negativity. Don't fall for it. Move out of that space. Surround yourself with people who speak about productive issues, discuss problem solving steps, and deliver meaningful results. The devil cannot exist in such a positive environment. The logic and wisdom are that: don't fight a whale in water, don't fight an eagle in the sky, and don't fight a green snake in green grass. Don't fight the enemy in their natural habitat. Move them to an unfamiliar territory. That movement may be mental, spiritual, or even physical.

I hope this book will give you the courage and motivation you need to surge after your dreams and live a purposeful life.

Affably Yours
Saikou Camara

Foreword

As an avid reader, entrepreneur, husband, father, and community member, I've relied on personal help and growth books to further my education and knowledge to help me over the last 20 plus years I have run my own business in the competitive world of Real Estate Sales. I've also employed a coach for over 18 years to learn many of the things that Saikou mentioned in "HUSTLE LIKE AN IMMIGRANT", So I'm keenly aware of some of the challenges that many of us deal with daily.

As we strive to succeed (remember success is personal and your definition may be different from someone else's) in a very fast-paced world, oftentimes the biggest huddle we all face is not going to come from the outside but rather from within ourselves. The biggest of which is believing in ourselves that success is for us. In "Hustle like an Immigrant" Mr. Saikou Camara gave us five wonderful chapters that each spelled out a step-by-step approach to building a life that is full of meaning and service to others and with God's help we can attain at the highest level of our own definition of what success mean to us individually.

The lesson in this book applies to all of us and not just immigrants. Go build the life of your dreams and ask God to guide you and then start running!

Sincerely
Ebrima Wadda
Windermere Real Estate, Seattle, WA, USA

Preface

I was born and raised in The Gambia, West Africa, the smallest country on mainland Africa and among the poorest in the world. I came to the United States of America shortly after completing high school with two hundred Gambian dalasi (an equivalent of about $5 U.S. at the time) in my pocket. I overcame the obstacles of this mammoth capitalist society to earn both my bachelor's and master's degrees in Computer Science. And almost two decades on, today I work as an experienced consulting network engineer for some of the Fortune 200 companies in corporate America. I also double down as a public speaker, a personal development coach, an entrepreneur, a four-time self-published author, and the founder and president of an international non-profit organization. My story is not any more special than any other underdog story you may have heard of, but it is a story that is uniquely characterized by my **why**, **what**, **self-discipline**, **perseverance**, and willingness to take **risks**. I call this the *Hustle Like an Immigrant* mindset. My life story is only an extension of that of many people before me who had to fight with their backs against the metaphorical wall. Through no choice of mine have I chosen to be born into challenging circumstances, and for that reason or that of lack of choice, have tried my hardest in living it the best possible way I could.

In 2012, a *Global Entrepreneurship Monitor* study, by Xavier et. al, reported that immigrants were more likely to start businesses than members of the native population in most of the 69 countries in the focus groups that were surveyed. For instance, in the United States, where 13.7% of the population is foreign-born, immigrants represent 20.2% of the self-employed workforce and 25% of startup founders. And according to a 2018 study by the National Foundation for American Policy, immigrants founded or co-founded 55% of the United States' billion-dollar companies - so-called unicorns, privately held startup companies with current valuation of 1 billion dollars or more.

If you were among the few privileged or lucky individuals to have received the COVID-19 vaccine, chances are you have an immigrant scientist or entrepreneur to thank for it. Because some of the key leaders involved in the vaccine research process, such as Pfizer, BioNTech, and Moderna who are pioneers in the field of mRNA-based vaccine research were all founded or cofounded by immigrants.

2016 studies by Mavletova et. al, *Is the Willingness to Take Risks Contagious? A comparison of Immigrants and Native-born in the United States*, found that people of immigrant background are more likely to take risks in venturing into new endeavors and achieving their goals or becoming success stories.

Arguably, the two most successful coaches in college sports, Nick Saban, football coach at Alabama, and Mike Krzyzewski, former basketball coach of Duke University, are both second-generation Americans, the grandsons of Eastern European immigrants who came to the United States and worked in coal mines. Nick Saban's paternal grandfather was born in Croatia. And both Mike's maternal and paternal grandparents were immigrants from Poland.

Bill Belichick, the greatest coach in the National Football League (NFL) history, is a second-generation American, his paternal grandparents were immigrants from Croatia.

The 44th and 45th presidents of the United States both had at least one biological immigrant parent. Barack Obama is a first generation American. His father was an international student from Kenya. And Donald Trump's paternal grandfather was an immigrant from Germany and his mother was an immigrant from Scotland.

Former Apple co-founder Steve Jobs's biological father is an immigrant from Syria, though Steve was given up for adoption to his adopted parents. The CEO and founder of Amazon, Jeff Bezos, got his last name from his adoptive father Miguel Bezos, an immigrant from Cuba. Elon Musk, the founder of SpaceX and CEO of Tesla, Inc., and the richest man in the world as of September of 2022, is an immigrant from Pretoria, South Africa.

America has a philosophical definition of success and attaining the American dream, where every citizen can be guaranteed equality, freedom, and material prosperity if they remain law-abiding and hardworking. In my opinion, this is the bedrock of the *Hustle Like an Immigrant* mentality. That every individual can become a success story irrespective of their background. This is no coincidence, because America is believed to be the land of immigrants where dreams can come true.

I didn't grow up with the belief that where or how I was born was going to define my final destiny. I grew up with this veracious quest for greatness. I always believe that my destiny is going to be far greater than the circumstances I was born in. This book is a challenge to all people to dare to dream beyond their imaginations. Be committed to some goal in your life, a mission, a purpose, or a calling. Something bigger than yourself that will become your motivating and comforting therapy.

Whatever your goals, dreams, and aspirations are, *Hustle like an Immigrant* should be able to guide you to achieve them.

Introduction

Many years ago, around my 6th grade, a young lady in our neighborhood said she was going to commit suicide by drowning herself in *Ndangan,* a small fishing area near the riverside in Old Jeshwang. She was consumed by and could no longer bear the shame of failing her 6th grade comprehensive exams called *common entrance.* A bunch of us neighborhood kids followed her to the riverside, not to stop her or offer her any help to persuade her from going through with it, but to watch her drown herself.

That may sound awful to many. But hold on now before you judge us as heartless evil kids. In retrospect, I'd like to argue that our behavior could be explained by our youthful innocence and ignorance, but that would be ingenuine. We were intrigued by the thought of someone taking their own life. That was unheard of and so foreign to our existence that we were more curious to watch what could have happened rather than being empathetic towards what was troubling her and her mental state.

Growing up in The Gambia, I saw poor people all around me, my family being one of them, but they had joy in their hearts. Except for clinically diagnosed mentally ill people, you don't see or hear about people taking their own lives no matter how difficult or tough life gets. No matter what trouble or hardship people go through, they maintain a sense of hope anchored on a faith-based system that God will make a way. It is a common dictum to hear our people say *Yallah Bakhna* (God is good/able). Where I'm from, ***hope*** saves lives.

I now live in a society where there is abundance of food, medicine, doctors, trained psychiatrist, and so on, yet we have a very high suicide rate. Per the American Foundation for Suicide Prevention (AFSP), The age-adjusted suicide rate in 2020 was 13.48 per 100,000 individuals. What I keep asking myself is what could possibly push people so far to the edge that they are willing to throw in the towel and give up on life? I have come to the realization that the human mind is very powerful and could be easily weaponized. When the human mind turns on itself, it is even worse, and it can lead to people causing great harm to themselves.

I profoundly believe that there exists in the human heart a propensity to hope, and the pressures of everyday life sometimes wear us down, drain our spirit, and require our hope to be restored. Restoring hope in people can help save their lives when their mind turns against them. I'm in the business of restoring and repairing hope for those I can impact positively.

Thankfully, the young lady never went through with her suicide plans. We all went to the riverside and watched her sit there and cry all day. We all walked back home together later in the evening, and we moved on. And almost three decades on, she is now older, married with kids, and living happily as ever.

The late pastor, Myles Munroe, best-selling author, and motivational speaker wielded a huge influence on millions of evangelical Christians and non-Christians alike, around the world. In his audiobook, *The Leadership Attitude of Lion & Eagle*, he narrated that there are only two animals on the planet that God identified Himself with. The first is the eagle and the second is the lion - both are the natural leaders of their respective habitat.

Pastor Munroe said that the eagle is the king of the bird family, and the lion is the king of the jungle. I will focus on his presentation on the leadership attributes of the lion. He said the lion has what he called "the spirit of leadership." In this context, the spirit of leadership refers to *attitude*. A leader has an attitude that makes him or her different from followers. In his explanation, he made this argument, and I couldn't agree with him more:

Number one: The lion is not the heaviest animal in the jungle. That will be the hippopotamus.

Number two: The lion is not the largest animal in the jungle. That will be the elephant.

Number three: The lion is not the fastest animal in the jungle. That will be the cheetah.

Number four: The lion is not the smartest animal in the jungle. That will be the Chimpanzee.

Number five: The lion is not the tallest animal in the jungle. That will be the giraffe.

However, ask anyone in this world, which animal is the *king* of the jungle, and they will say - the *lion*. When he shows up, all the other animals run away. The lion is unequivocally accepted and recognized by people as the KING of the jungle. What makes the lion different from all other animals? Elephants are stronger than lions, cheetahs & leopards are faster than lions, and lions cannot beat tigers in a fight. Also, crocodiles and alligators are nearly immortal creatures according to recent studies, as they do not have a defined lifespan. This means that instead of having an average or defined lifespan, they are more likely to die from accidents, disease, predation, or starvation instead of old age. But all these animals fear the lion. The lion has a commanding attitude that causes every other animal to be afraid of it.

What makes these massive animals respect such a small cat? The attitude and belief system of the lion is the difference. For example, a lion will see an elephant and one word that comes to its mind is *food*, "I can eat this thing", and he acts the way he thinks. In the same scenario, the elephant is bigger, stronger, smarter, and more powerful but when it sees the lion one word that comes to its mind is *predator*, "this beast can eat me" and it tries to run away from it.

In essence, attitude is the product of belief. You cannot have an attitude beyond your belief. Your attitude comes from your belief system. The lion is the king because of what he believes about himself.

America is widely accepted as the greatest country in the world. Even the citizens of its biggest rivals such as China and Russia accept the United States of America as the greatest nation in the world. However, this is not supported by facts. The most educated country in the world, as of September of 2022, is Canada. The smartest country in the world in terms of IQ, as of September of 2022, is Japan. The wealthiest country in the world in terms of per capita, as of September of 2022, is Qatar. The largest country in the world is Russia. And the country with the largest population in the world, as of July of 2022, is China. But ask anyone around the world, including Americans themselves, which country is the greatest nation in the world, and the majority of the people will say the *United States of America.*

You must first believe in yourself for anything to work. Man is a product of his beliefs. So you believe, so you are. And that is the *Hustle Like an Immigrant* mindset.

Hustle like an Immigrant is not an attack towards nativism, it is a celebration of triumph born out of desperation and necessity. Anyone who ever had to make sacrifices and fight relentlessly to achieve a goal or dream bigger than themselves can relate to this doctrine.

People often ask me with some sense of skepticism what *Hustle Like an Immigrant* is all about. *Hustle Like an Immigrant* is a guide to assist everyday ordinary people to reach their highest potential. The first thing to recognize about it is that it is a **mindset**.

This mindset can be learned, and it can be taught. It has nothing to do with nationality, ethnicity, tribe, race, sex, gender, age, or creed. It is a mentality, it-*factor*, that we are all inherently born with. All we need is to have someone or something, be it an event or life circumstance to trigger us and allow us to tap into it and unlock the mindset. It just happens to be that when people get out of their comfort zones and their backs are now against a metaphorical wall, they often find themselves digging deeper within themselves and triggering that *it-factor* switch on either intentionally or out of necessity. But for everyone else, allow this book to be the triggering motive for you, your guide, to unearthing, mining, and discovering the hustler spirit buried deep down in your core.

Canadian Entrepreneur, Mark J. Quann, the author of *Rich Man, Poor Bank,* stated that immigrants are four times more likely to become millionaires in the United States. In essence, being an immigrant in the United States gives you a competitive advantage to succeed in comparison to born natives. It is no coincidence that this is the case, and it has everything to do with the mindset.

Everywhere I have traveled to, I have witnessed immigrants turn their nightmares into dreams and their dreams into accomplished goals. They turned scarcity into abundance. They triumphed over obstacles to get to success. Success in this context goes beyond financial success alone. Success here is three-dimensional: wealth, health, and spirituality. You will note that the word success does not come in measurements. It is neither big nor small. I have credited this success to five qualities that all successful people everywhere possess: Your **why**, your **what**, your **discipline**, your **perseverance**, and your willingness to take **risks**.

1
Your Why

"When you find your WHY, you don't hit snooze no more! You find a way to make it happen"
- Eric Thomas

Christopher McDougall, in his book, *Born to Run*, shared an adage about something amazing that happens in Africa every morning in the jungle. The story goes - every morning in Africa a gazelle wakes up, it knows it must outrun the fastest lion or it will become breakfast. Also, every morning in Africa, a lion wakes up, it knows it must run faster than the slowest gazelle, or it will starve. Therefore, it doesn't matter whether you're the lion or a gazelle - when the sun comes up in Africa, you'd better be running. And whosoever has the strongest *why* wins the day. If the gazelle's quest for survival is stronger than the lion's hunger, the gazelle lives. But if the lion's taste for blood and hunger is stronger than the gazelle's motivation to run for its life, it becomes a meal for the lion.

Buddha said your purpose in life is to find your purpose! Deeds alone without a purpose are meaningless.

The first step, the genesis of *Hustle Like an Immigrant* mindset is discovering your purpose. Your *why*. It was German philosopher Frederick Nietzsche who said, "he who has a why can endure any how". But I will go further and say he who has a **strong** *why* can overcome any obstacle. The word strong here is relative depending on one's commitment and conviction. Find any immigrant in this world and ask them why they come to where they are, and I promise you that you will hear a captivating story that will most likely inspire you.

For many African migrants overseas, working abroad is no paradise because they are separated from their families. Whether crazy rich, dirt poor, or middle class, these migrants know sacrifice. Africans in the diaspora have always worked so hard that they become disoriented or almost repulsed by the concept of personal happiness. It is a cross they bear, but it is also an intrinsic trait that defines them and makes them who they are - the families and loved ones they left behind are their constant motivation. That is what is important to them. And everything they do or work for is for their families back home. Many people in Africa consider them as unsung heroes and rightly so because the dollar remittances they send home keep many African countries' economies afloat. According to the World Bank, in 2019, global remittances to Sub-Saharan Africa (SSA) reached an all-time high of $48B. Nigeria, which has a sizable diaspora across the world, is by far the largest recipient of remittance flows with $23.8 billion in 2019, followed by Ghana, $3.5 billion, and Kenya, $2.8 billion. In South Sudan, remittances of $1.3 billion accounted for 34% of its GDP, the highest in the region.

This predicament is not peculiar to African immigrants. It is true about many immigrants from other parts of the world as well, especially immigrants from third world countries residing in developed countries.

African immigrants in the U.S have also shown to have more college education and higher rate of degree attainment compared to any other groups. 49% of all African immigrants hold college degrees in America, according to studies conducted by the journal of Blacks in Higher Education and the Harvard Educational Review, in 2001. African immigrants obtain a degree at a rate twice higher than U.S born Caucasians and four times higher than that of African Americans, according to the 2000 Census. These unprecedented achievements are not accidental. They are inspired by the clarity of purpose many of the African immigrants arrived in America with. The survival of their extended families is directly tied to their individual attainment of success. It is incumbent upon them to succeed at all costs.

People who know their *why* often have a sense of clarity and become laser-focused on their goals.

These are five key activities you can use to identify your *why*:

Identify the Things About Yourself that are Bigger than You:

If I ask you, my readers, to run through a glass door you will look at me crazy. But if your loved ones, be it your children, spouse, siblings, or parents are trapped in a burning building and I ask you to run through a brick wall to save them, you won't hesitate. This is because your *how* and *what* are dictated by your *why*. No matter how ambitious you are, no matter how self-motivated you are, you will come across obstacles in life that are bigger and stronger than you and they will likely knock you down. Unless you have a bigger and stronger *why* than the obstacles you will face, you will not be able to muster the courage to get back up on your feet to keep fighting and advancing forward.

On February 11, 1990, Buster Douglas, who was perceived as a nobody in the boxing world, pulled off one of the biggest upsets in sports history. Douglas was a huge underdog but knocked out Mike Tyson (Iron Mike) who was at the height of his career, in the 10th round of their world heavyweight championship boxing match in Tokyo.

When Mike Tyson landed in Tokyo in January of 1990 to defend his world title against Buster Douglas, the bout was seen as a complete walk-over - some bookmakers even refused to take bets on the fight. The Mirage, the only casino in Las Vegas, bold enough to offer odds to punters, rated Douglas as a 42-1 underdog. Basically, those wanting to bet on the fight were told to not place a bet in favor of a Douglas upset.

What the boxing world didn't know at the time was that though Mike was evidently the better fighter and clear favorite to win the fight, they didn't know the psyche of the two fighters at the time. Mike will later narrate in his autobiography that "On January 8, 1990, I got aboard a plane to fly to Tokyo," he wrote. "Kicking and screaming. I didn't want to fight; all I was interested in then was partying and fucking women. I didn't consider Buster Douglas much of a challenge. I didn't even bother watching any of his fights on video." He continued, "I had easily beaten everybody who had knocked him out." Tyson even confessed to sleeping with some hotel maids, including threesomes, nights before the big bout.

Unfortunately for him, those affairs would be the last time he enjoyed success in Tokyo as the world witnessed one of the biggest sporting upsets in history. On the other hand, just weeks before the big bout, Douglas's mother, Lula, suffered a stroke and died at the age of 46. Douglas was very close to his mother, and he was still hurting as he entered the ring for the biggest fight of his life.

An unprepared and unfocussed Iron Mike was still a heck of a fighter. After cumbersomely following the challenger on wobbly legs until the eighth round, Mike Tyson's trademark right uppercut landed on Douglas chins and sent him flying on the canvas, seemingly Douglas was finished. The entire boxing world watched in disbelief that it took Iron Mike all the way to the eight round to drop Douglas. Then something unexpected happened. Douglas got to his feet at the count of nine and the round ended just after that. Nobody had ever recovered from a Mike Tyson uppercut knock down up to that moment. The spectators were in awe.

Douglas went on to drop Tyson to the canvas with a flurry of punches in the 10th round and the Iron Mike was unable to get back to his feet before the 10-count ending the fight. Tyson, who was 37-0 at the time with 33 of those wins coming by knockout, had never even been knocked down in his career.

After the big fight, the question that every spectator wanted to know was: what was Buster Douglas's motivation during the fight? How did he recover from an Iron Mike uppercut punch that sent him to the canvas? And he said in the post-match interview that before his mother passed away, she had told all her friends that her son was going to defeat Mike Tyson and he wasn't going to let her down as she watched over him from heaven.

While Mike Tyson didn't have a reason to fight Douglas, Douglas had a heavenly reason to see to it that he defeats Mike. His *why* was way stronger than Mike's *why* or lack thereof.

What Makes You Come Alive?

Your *why* must be something personal to you. The question, "what is your why?" requires you to be introspective and answer some questions about your personal experiences to uncover your life's purpose. It doesn't have to make sense or be meaningful to other people. It just needs to be meaningful to you.

On Jan. 21, 1997, Michael Jordan had a monster game against the New York Knicks. Jordan ultimately scored 51 points for the Chicago Bulls as they defeated the Knicks 88-87. He said he was motivated by the then New York Knicks coach, Jeff Van Gundy's pregame comments. Van Gundy alluded that Jordan cons other opposing players by befriending them and beating them on the court. To Jordan, these comments seemed to have downplayed the high level of work ethic and standard he put into his craft. Many people didn't consider Van Gundy's comments as extremely offensive at the time. However, Jordan didn't take Jeff's comments lightly. He felt like his hard work and integrity as a man and a professional was put into question by being called a con artist. He used those comments as his motivation. He played that night and the rest of that season with a vendetta, a score-to-settle mentality, and ultimately won the NBA 1996-1997 season championship and was named the finals' most valuable player (MVP).

When Kobe Bryant died in 2020, his widow, Vanessa Bryant delivered a very touching and emotional speech. Mrs. Bryant said: "One of the reasons why my husband played through injuries and pain was because he remembered being a little kid, sitting in the nosebleeds with his dad and watching his favorite player play." As Vanessa was uttering these words, she turned to Jordan who attended the funeral. "I remember asking him why he couldn't just sit a game out because he was hurting. He said, 'What about the fans that saved up to watch me play just once?' Kobe never forgot about his fans. If he could help it, he would play every minute of every game. He loved you all so much." Mrs. Bryant concluded. Kobe's *why* was to always give his fans 100% effort, irrespective of what he was personally dealing with. He never wanted to cheat his fans. And that personal commitment delivered five NBA championships in his playing career.

People who are emotionally motivated by their *why*, no matter how insignificant it may seem to others, usually have a competitive advantage over other people.

What is Important to You:

My *why* stemmed from an early childhood experience I first shared in my inaugural book, *Testimony of an African Immigrant - A Promise to my Father*.

There was a time when my *why* was motivated by my obsession to be addressed as Mr. Camara. When I was in the

3rd grade at Albion Primary School in Banjul, the capital city of The Gambia, my class teacher had one day asked all the students to tell our parents to report to school for a Parents-Teacher meeting. When I arrived with my dad, I remembered my 3rd grade teacher standing at the school gate welcoming all our parents. She addressed the parents of the other students with their proper salutations; Mr. Njie, Mr. Jones, Mr. Ceesay, Mr. Daniel, Mr. Jobe, and when she got to my dad, she casually just addressed him as "Camara". The parents of the other pupils were dressed in very nice European-style attires (nice button-up shirts, neckties, jackets, etc.), and my dad was dressed in his local African attire called *Haftan*. My dad had no formal western education, but he was well versed in the Quran. He could read and write in Arabic. I was filled with mixed emotions. I was angry and embarrassed at the same time. I was not ashamed of my dad and never have I ever felt ashamed of him in my life. He was an honorable and respectable elder in my community.

When newlyweds had issues in their marriages, they used to consult with my father for his advice. When people die, he used to be asked to come and pray for them. When babies were born, he used to be invited to usher them into this world with his blessings. And when other families had financial problems, he shared the little money he had with them. As a small entrepreneur, he had traveled to many different countries, and he was a very cultured man. Not once did it ever occur to me that he was a lesser individual in the presence of his contemporaries due to his lack of western education. However, that evening I realized that he might have been an elderly statesman in my small local community, but to my teacher and everybody like her, he was just a man identified as "Camara". I was embarrassed that my teacher didn't accord my father the proper respect I thought he deserved. After the meeting, I couldn't stop thinking about it and I confronted my dad for allowing my teacher to address him as just "Camara" and not Mr. Camara.

My father has always been like this immortal superhero figure to me who can do all things. That was the first time in my life I saw mortality in his eyes. He looked at me in the eyes, wagering his fingers in my face, and his voice shaky, and he said to me (in Mandingo) in a very somber voice, *"If your friends' parents are wealthier and more educated than me and your mother, that is no fault of yours. But if your friends became more educated or successful than you someday - that would be your fault. Your mother and I will try everything within our means to give you an equal opportunity so that one day you will not just be addressed as Camara. your teacher and everybody else will address you as Mr. Camara."*

At the time I was not satisfied with his answer but one thing you do not do as an African is to question your African parents, not even once, let alone twice.

Few months later, my teacher asked the class what we would want to be when we grow up. To her credit, she was trying to inspire us and motivate us to dream and set goals. Some of my classmates responded, president, lawyer, doctor, police officer, professional athletes, teacher, and when she got to me, I said, *"A mister"* *"A Mister?"* She replied. *"But you can still be called a mister and have a professional career like an office clerk"*. I said to her *I don't know what an office clerk does, but I know what a mister is. A mister is respected in his community.* Unlike the parents of the other students in my school, my parents didn't have any formal western education. I didn't have a professional role model at the time. I didn't know what a lawyer does or what it takes to become a doctor or an engineer. I was only motivated by the anger of my dad not getting the proper respect of a third-grade teacher just because he couldn't speak English and was not dressed in nice Western attire. It was never my childhood dream to acquire a master's degree in computer science or pursue a career in the engineering discipline. All I ever wanted was to keep the promise that I made to my father, that someday I will be addressed as Mr. Camara.

That encounter in my third grade was a significant moment in my early life, it motivated me throughout my formative years, and in 2004, I arrived in America with an unwavering *why*, five bucks in my pocket, a small suitcase filled with few clothes, and an unrelenting audacity to succeed.

What Will You Do Without a Paycheck:

Do you work for a living to feed your soul, or do you work for a paycheck? If you are doing something that you are passionate about, you will be able to do it for the rest of your life and it won't feel like work. There will never be a Sunday night where you are dreading the imminent Monday morning.

You need to find something that makes you tick in the morning when you do not feel like waking up. If your only motivation for going to the gym is to have a six pack or flat tummy, firm buttocks, or a sizzle physique, then you may not go to the gym on the days you do not feel like working out. But if your reason for working out is motivated by wellness to keep yourself healthy and possibly prolong your life span for your children or family, you will always find a reason to go to the gym. If your only reason for working in your profession is for money, not to say money is not a good enough reason, but if you have extra money somewhere and you can afford not to go to work, then you may not go to work when you do not feel like it.

Money should only be a *satisfier* and not the main motivation. If you are an engineer and your reason for your passion is that you see yourself as a problem solver and the world needs you, you don't just say I don't feel like solving problems today. If you are a doctor or a nurse and your reason is not just to get a paycheck but to save lives, you don't just say "today I don't feel like saving lives", because other peoples' lives depend on you. If you are a lawyer and your reason for being in the legal profession is to ensure that justice prevail and your absence could mean injustice or miscarriage of justice towards an innocent person, you don't just say "I don't feel like working today".

If people choose a more meaningful reason for going into their professions, the world will be a better place. I am challenging you to see yourself a little bit more significant in your professions, and if you are still unsure or confused about your *why*, here is a little reminder. Lawyers should be defenders of justice, farmers should be nation feeders, doctors and nurses should be healers, men and women in uniform should be nation defenders and crusaders, accountants and economists should be anti-corruption agents, and entertainers should be the joy of our universe, and so on. You are more than just an employee, civil servant, or a worker, your society needs you, your community needs you, and the world needs you.

What Would You be Doing if You Learned that You Only had a Year to Live:

If the angel of death visits you tonight and asks you to give a reason why you should live for one more day, why you should continue occupying the universe - what will you say? What is your life worth? Is your life only worth your daily job? Is your life only worth being a husband or wife? Is your life only worth being someone else's child? Is your life only worth being a parent? What is your life worth? I hope this encourages you to do some soul searching. Find the meaning and purpose of your life and pursue it. Don't just be a name. Don't just be a living organism occupying space and existing in this universe. Live a meaningful life. Live a purposeful life.

Whatever your faith is, serve your God and uplift mankind. Do not lose your soul over vanity. You should always have a bigger purpose than yourself. A 2015 study, "Prosociality enhances meaning in life" revealed that having a purpose in life leads to a longer lifespan in older adults (Daryl, et al). It further suggests that altruistically motivated prosociality – acting in ways that benefits others – is a self-transcending action that may provide meaning in life.

Find your purpose and live your creed. Your dreams, ideas, goals, aspirations may change the world. Don't be selfish, live your true potential for the greater you and for the greater good.

2
Your What

---

*"It must be borne in mind that the tragedy of life
doesn't lie in not reaching your goal.
The tragedy lies in having no goals to reach."*
- Benjamin E. Mays

People without goals are often used by people with goals. The second step of *Hustle Like an Immigrant* mindset is setting up goals. Your *what* in this book refers to your goals. Until you become thoroughly immersed in your life goals and ambitions, you won't realize them, you must commit in body, mind, and spirit. You must go all in on your goals.

The *Hustle Like an Immigrant* five key steps of Goals Setting are:

Identify and Define Your Goals:

Many people cannot identify or define their goals. One must identify goals that really motivate them and keep them going. If you've thoughtfully considered the areas of your life where you want to accomplish something, you should find goals that truly motivate you.

As I reflect upon my childhood story, I see glimpses of my goals even though I didn't know them as such at the time. I wanted to earn the respect of society by attaining higher education. As I got older, my life goals began to grow along and became more refined. I began to realize that in order to be a respectable member of society, there are other checklists one must complete. These checklists became my motivating factor, in essence, they were my *why* and to achieve them, I needed to attain a specific level of education. I also needed to carry myself in a certain way and become a responsible member of my community. Moreover, I needed to positively impact my community through community service, and so on. My *why* (purpose) laid the foundation stones upon which I could clearly define my *what* (goals). If you have a very strong *why*, it should help lead you to your *what*.

Well defined goals give you direction. Have you ever wondered how a plane can fly through the clouds from America to Asia and make it to its destination, but you can barely find the nearest gas station in a different city on your own without the use of a GPS? The difference is called direction. A plane knows where it is going, how to get there, and what time to get there. If a plane is not programmed, or worst case, programmed with the wrong information, it will get lost.

In March of 2019, a British Airline flight took off from London City Airport and was supposed to be headed to Dusseldorf, Germany. That was the plan, but instead, the plane ended up taking off in the opposite direction and landed in Edinburgh, 525 miles away from its intended destination! According to the airline, the incorrect flight plan was filed by WDL Aviation, which operated the flight on behalf of British Airways. Many people know their destinations, but they lack direction. Clearly defined goals in one's life, provide direction and ensure a proper take-off and landing.

You must identify your short term, midterm, and long-term goals. Your short-term goals are things you want to achieve in the immediate near future, such as working out consistently, finishing a *do it yourself* (DIY) project in your home, quitting smoking, etc. Your medium-term goals are things that will take a little bit longer to attain, such as finding a job while going to school, learning a new skill, changing your diet, etc. And your long-term goals are things that will take you years to achieve, such as completing a four-year college or university degree program, getting married and having children, learning a foreign language, becoming a business mogul, etc. You must define your daily, weekly, monthly, yearly, and decade-long goals to help you always focus on your *what*.

Write Down Your Goals:

I have my own arsenal of techniques for setting and reaching my goals, but the best goal setting practices start with being crystal clear about what you want and then the next step is writing them down. Everyone needs to have well defined written goals. Be it life goals, daily work, financial, healthy lifestyle, relationship, spirituality goals, or whatever it may be. Writing down your goals makes them easier to attain and manage, in fact, this practice creates self-accountability. It brings to mind the Latin proverb *Verba volant, scripta manent,* which literally means "spoken words fly away, written words remain".

In fact, per a study conducted by Dave Kohl, professor emeritus who served the Virginia Tech Department of Agricultural and Applied Economics from 1978 until his retirement in 2003, reported that people who regularly write down their goals earn nine times as much over their lifetimes as the people who do not. The same study shows that 80% of Americans say they don't have goals, and 16% say they do have goals but don't write them down, with less than 4% write down their goals, and fewer than 1% review them on an ongoing basis. People who write down their goals are 33% more likely to achieve them. Writing your goals down not only forces you to get clear on exactly what you want, doing so also plays a part in motivating you to complete the tasks necessary to successfully accomplish said goals.

In 1997, Jim Carrey spoke with Oprah Winfrey about his struggle days and manifesting his goal by writing himself a check for $10 million, which he dated Thanksgiving 1995, which is celebrated on the last Thursday of November every year in the U.S. Carrey explained, "I wrote myself a check for $10 million for 'acting services rendered' and I gave myself five years... or three years maybe. I dated it Thanksgiving 1995 and I put it in my wallet, and I kept it there and it deteriorated and deteriorated. But then, just before Thanksgiving 1995, I found out that I was going to make $10 million on Dumb and Dumber." At the time he wrote the check, Carrey certainly wasn't earning that level of income, but he knew if he wrote the check to himself and took the steps to reach that goal, he could certainly achieve the success he dreamed about. In essence, he manifested his goals into the universe. The act of writing down your goals is a form of manifestation. Manifesting your goals by writing them down helps you to understand that it is not magic, it is a process. It makes your goals tangible and infuses life into them. This process can feel effortless if done right.

Research Your Goals:

Do some research. Think about your goals and dreams, and then learn more about them. Find out how other people who have achieved similar goals developed themselves for the tasks ahead or career you want. If you lack the skills for the career you are interested in, consider job shadowing or an unpaid internship. Attend workshops. Read books. Ask yourself these key questions:

What kind of training, education and skills are required?

What are the real-life work conditions, the work environment, the work schedule, and the constraints?

What are the likely rewards and accolades, for example: medals, salary, trophies, fringe benefits, room to grow, retirement plans, etc.?

Are these rewards and accolades important to you or worth your while?

If you genuinely find the answers to these questions, you should be well prepared to undertake any task required.

Set Deadlines and Milestones:

First, ensure that you have done your due diligence, by writing some very smart and well-thought-out goals that you have researched about and are in line with your overall objective(s). After which, you then need to establish a time frame that works for each goal and start living it with every decision you make, because your actions and decisions must reflect and be consistent with your goals.

Identify milestones with measurable and attainable outcomes. When you define milestones for yourself, you build a strong ladder towards your goals. The more rungs you add to the ladder, the easier the climb. This can be done in phases, quarters, or major milestones. If you are struggling to set and stick to your milestones, don't give up, get an accountability partner. Make sure it's someone who will be firm but fair with you, like a family member or a close friend. The goal is not to beat you down, but to keep you honest and focused on the main task. You will soon be able to look back and see how far you've come.

Review Your Goals:

The final step in setting goals is to frequently review them. When you set goals, they should always meet these five criteria: *Specific, Relevant, Measurable, Attainable, and Time Bound.*

Specific: Your goals must be clear and well-defined to keep you focused. If you have goals of becoming a dentist, write *I want to become a dentist*, don't just say I want to be a doctor. That is not specific enough.

Relevant: Your goals must be relevant to your life. If you have no interest in basketball, maybe you shouldn't have a goal to become a basketball coach.

Measurable: Your goals must have precise expected outcomes and dates to keep you accountable and on track.

Attainable: Your goals must be achievable. Setting impossible goals such as walking on foot from the U.S. to China can be a futile endeavor.

Time Bound: Your goals must have a final completion deadline to avoid procrastinating on them for eternity.

Having goals is the most selfish thing (or self-rewarding as I like to call it) you can ever do. Be prepared to be talked about and misunderstood as you go through the process of realizing and attaining your goals. Your goals will eventually dictate your entire life (or lifestyle). Your goals will determine the type of food you eat, the time you will go to bed, the time you wake up, and even the kind of friends you keep.

Speaking of friends, if it is true that birds of a feather flock together, then some people will become successful in life as soon as they change their immediate circle. Some people are eagles but flock with pigeons. You cannot win with the wrong team. If you are the wisest or smartest member of your team or your friend circle, you need to either help them level up to your standards or you will inevitably outgrow your team. If you are hanging around nine unmotivated people, chances are you will become the 10th unmotivated member of the group. Many people, especially young people, have their goals derailed not because they aren't smart or good enough, but because they keep the wrong crowd around them. They've allowed friends who have no deeper understanding or vested interest in their life to dictate how they live.

I have realized that so many people are short of greatness only because the people they surround themselves with keep telling them that "you have done enough". They limit them from pushing a little bit further, work a little bit harder, study a little bit longer, practice a little bit tougher. They psychologically make them feel content and accomplished. Some of you will become successful when you stop listening to too many compliments. Dwarfs cannot compliment other dwarfs' height - they are all dwarfs. Surround yourself with people who push you to your limits and some more.

Your feelings determine how you think. If you want to think success and be positive, be around people who make you and keep you always feeling hungry and positive. This will help you maintain a certain level of expectation and demand for excellence towards your work. Some people are not successful because their brains are cluttered with negative distractions due to the environment and the people they surround themselves with. Humans are emotional beings. Control and protect your emotions from negative energy and distractions. Your success depends on it. Energy cannot be destroyed - it can only be transferred. That's basic physics.

3

Discipline

"Do not be out work[ed]"

-Kobe Bryant

Once you know your *why* or purpose and set your *what* or goals. The third step of the *Hussle Like an Immigrant* mindset is *discipline* or self-discipline. The most successful people in the world are self-disciplined. I believe self-discipline is a set of self-assigned principles that guide and support you to achieve high-yield results.

I once listened to Bill Gates talk about his work ethic. He said he didn't take a vacation, not even once, in his entire twenties because he was too busy building Microsoft. I am not saying that you do not need to rest or have some personal time off and a healthy work-life balance. But the *Hustle Like an Immigrant* mentality dictates that you do not rest when you get tired. You rest when you're done with your task.

What are your values? They can be the principles, standards or beliefs that are sacred to you that you find most worthwhile. You probably already have a core set of beliefs that guide you. Be it religious beliefs or cultural norms. But if you don't, you need some for your self-discipline and continuous improvement. I call them values. These are the steps for a disciplined lifestyle:

Be Self-Accountable:

Self-discipline is about accountability. How do you hold yourself accountable for the things you said you are going to do? Accountability is a habit, and it starts with the small things. If you make a promise to yourself that you will clean your dishes before the end of the day, and it is 11:59pm and your dishes are still sitting in the kitchen sink, what do you do? Do you just dismiss it and try to do them another day or do you hold yourself accountable and not go to bed until you do the dishes?

Here is a small exercise I practice in my life daily to hold myself accountable. I promised myself that I will either go to the gym or run three miles (5k's) every weekday before I retire to bed. I do this because I understand that the mental benefits of fitness outweigh the physical benefits. Physical fitness is not about a perfect body, it's about feeling healthy including having a healthy state of mind. And any day I fail to run my miles or complete my workouts, I do not eat supper for that day. Let me be the first to tell you that I love my dinners, I love food, my mouth is getting watery now just talking about dinner. If I break the promise I made to myself - I hold myself accountable for it. Accountability is a necessary ingredient for success. We punish our children by holding them accountable for their actions. We take away their TV time, play times, toys, etc. whenever they violate rules, we put in place for them. But as adults and parents we often violate our own rules without accountability for our actions.

Every year I see people make New Year's resolutions that they will make changes in their lives: They will lose weight, they will start working out regularly, they will eat healthy, they will go back to school, they will become better people, they will become better parents, they will become closer to their god(s) by praying or meditating more often, they will start their own business, and so on. By Valentine's Day, they have already given up on all their promises because there is no accountability if they failed to keep their promise to themselves. Applying the principles of self-discipline and accountability will guide you to achieve high-yield results you set out to accomplish.

Aspire for Greatness in Everything You Do and Practice Hard:

Successful people don't aspire for greatness in a quest for immortality or vanity. Aspiring for greatness is not the end-product or finish line that matters. It is the process and journey to greatness that is worthwhile. Show me what you are doing today, and I'll predict your tomorrow. You are where you are today (good or bad) because of what you did yesterday. Take a good look at what you are doing today because that will be your tomorrow. We may all have dreams and goals - the only difference is that some people dream in their sleep while others dream with their eyes wide open.

"When you practice, you get better. It's very simple." – Philip Glass

A friend of mine once told me that he is not good at writing. I asked him if he has ever written anything outside of schoolwork, a job application, or social media commentary? And he said no. I often hear people say I'm not good at math, I'm not good at writing, I'm not good with computers, etc., but they have never studied or practiced what they are not good at. I dare you to practice what you are not good at every day for six months and see if you will not become good at it. As the saying goes, *practice makes perfect*, no scratch that - that is a fallacy, nothing is perfect, practice makes improvement.

Jim Rohn once said becoming successful is easy, but it's a whole lot easier to be unsuccessful. It is easy to earn a college degree, but it is a whole lot easier not to go to school. It is easy to start a business and be your own CEO, but it is a whole lot easier to just be an employee. It is easy to lose weight but is a whole lot easier not to lose weight. Don't do what is easier to do, do what is necessary at any given moment.

Be Committed and Consistent:

Practice the discipline of repetition and consistency with the same enthusiasm. If you are going to chase your dreams and goals, you must understand that they may outrun you sometimes, but if you are stubbornly persistent and stay with the race, you will catch up. One thing I have learned recently is that effort is a neutralizing force. Whether you are a young man or a woman, whether you are blessed with skills, talents, knowledge, or whatnot. We all have what I call "E" for effort within us. That is our natural gift from nature. Never ever fail to make an effort and to try your best.

I personally encourage people to pray. I sometimes even endorse people surrendering their troubles to their god. But prayers without effort and action is superstition and witch-craft in my opinion. Get off your knees and stand on your feet and pray. Even the pastors who lead prayers on Sundays, wake up every morning to make their own breakfast. Manna will not fall from the skies.

The process of attaining success in anything is not for the faint of heart. The hard work, the late nights, and the battle to stick to a goal and not give in to self-doubt are the main ingredients. You must be committed to self-development practices. You are not fully committed to your goals until you begin to do things without the immediate expectation for a check. Money should not be the motivation - it should be the satisfier. I had watched over 10,000 hours of motivational videos on YouTube before I ever had my first paid public speaking opportunity. It just goes to show that hard work is the single most important ingredient to success. Don't skip the steps, go through the long process and you will be better for it.

Never give up on your goals, but remember that you must dig for gold in places where you can find gold. Being committed and consistently working on the wrong endeavor will not yield positive results. Some people cannot realize their dreams quite yet because they are looking in the wrong places or choosing the wrong career or profession, relationship, partner, and you name it.

Your Work Ethic Should Match Your Goals/Ambitions:

Your hustle or work ethic must match your ambitions. You cannot have a goal of becoming a professional athlete and don't go to the gym/court/tracks/field to practice. You cannot have a goal of becoming a lawyer and hate reading books. You cannot have a goal of becoming a bikini model and not look after your body. Your goals must match your lifestyle.

You must be obsessed with your dreams. I don't go to sleep because it's nighttime. I go to sleep when I'm done for the day. And often, I find myself awake and not done with my task at 6am in the morning.

Keep yourself busy with positive habits. An idle mind is the devil's playground. But constant busyness does not mean or translate to success. Work smartly and strategically. Make time for those who love you and you love. Do not get involved with things that do not concern you. Mind your business and stay focused on your own personal goals. Put your right hand up and say with me - ***"I solemnly swear to mind my business, my whole business, and nothing but my business, so help me God!"***

Ignore the Noise and Focus on the Task:

Learn to live beyond the opinions of others. Goal-oriented people are usually very focused. People may sometimes confuse your confidence and principles with arrogance, and your wild dreams and ambitions with craziness. But that is ok, just be yourself. People may know your last name, but they don't know your truth. Your truth is uniquely identified and characterized by your struggles and triumphs lived through your eyes. Own your truth, embrace your truth, and live your truth unapologetically.

I was at a friend's garden the other day, and I noticed that he had weeds all over his garden even though he didn't plant them. I realized that weeds do not need any caring or support to grow. They grow against all odds. Heck, I saw weeds growing out of concrete for heaven's sake. That's how stubborn weeds are. That is how negativity is like in life. Negativity needs no encouragement or support, it just grows. Stop wasting your time watering the negativity in your life and focus on your crops. Positivity, like crops, needs nurturing and caring to grow. **Critics will always have an opinion, and often, that's none of your business.**

According to Renaissance art historian Giorgio Vasari, Michelangelo's sculpture of David, a Biblical hero, is a symbol of the city of Florence, and is one of the masterpieces of art history and the universal symbol of sculpture and grandeur of Michelangelo. However, a Florentine official got an early look at it and commented that his nose seemed too big. I'm not sure if this story is true. It's difficult to know with many of Vasari's tales. However, I like it because there's an essential truth to it about people not really knowing what they're talking about.

Everyone was a critic in Renaissance Florence. While citizens agreed in 1504 that Michelangelo's David was a masterpiece, a few local artists carped that there were flaws in the statue – the right hand was a touch too big, the neck a little bit too long, the left shin oversized and something about the left buttock was not quite right. Piero Soderino, the head of the powerful Florentine Republic, also told the famously irascible Michelangelo that David's nose was too large. Michelangelo obviously didn't agree, but I guess this official was too important to say no to. Michelangelo then hid some marble dust in his hand, climbed back up his ladder and pretended to do some more chiseling on the offending proboscis. While he did so, he let some marble dust fall from his hand. The pompous Soderino was fooled – he examined the unchanged nose and announced it was much improved and far more "life-like." In reality, nothing had changed. The David sculpture is about 17 feet high, so the official wouldn't have been able to clearly see what Michelangelo did. But the wisdom in this story is that everyone has an opinion. Do not allow people's opinion of your gift or craft to make you alter your master-piece just because they have the privilege and opportunity to criticize you and or your work.

The job of the pessimist is to see the worst aspect in all situations. That is their job. They believe that this world is evil, and we are all doomed by destiny. They are drenched in negativity. The job of the optimist is to see hope and possibil-ities in all situations. That is their job. They share a positive belief that good will ultimately triumph over evil. They are drenched in positivity. Whether you are a pessimist or an op-timist, just do your job. But if you give me a choice to pick one doctrine, I'll rather be an optimist.

Someone somewhere thinks that you are the greatest thing ever since the advent of the iPhone. You have no business wasting your energy and time trying to impress or convince people who do not believe in you or think much of you. Know your worth and focus your time and energy on people who are willing to pay for your full price without negotiating or bargaining.

Stay away from doomsayers and naysayers, you can't win with them. Cut them off from your life. Positive reinforcement can change one's perspective and motivate them to achieve great things in life. There are plenty of good things happening around the world. Don't let anyone narrow your worldview based on their unhappiness or pessimistic views. Everyone should have at least two positive and happy souls they can always rely on, to uplift their spirit and soul when things look gloomy.

Master the Difference Between Value and Time:

What are you worth? In real estate the value of your house is not determined by only how nice or expensive your house is, but also the value of all the other houses in your neighborhood. Who is in your surroundings, are they adding or reducing your value? The company you keep around you can either increase or hurt your value.

If you know your worth and your purpose, you will never ever be afraid to walk away from individuals or groups who do not respect and value your worth and purpose. You will walk away from anyone who is out to hinder you from meeting your goals. You will walk away and never look back.

One of my mentees once called me and told me that she is contemplating quitting her job because she had not gotten a promotion in four years. I asked her why she thought she deserves a promotion, and she said because she has been in the same position in her place of employment for four years. I informed her that she had mistaken her time spent on her job for her worth.

On average, a doctor and a nurse spend approximately the same amount of time in a hospital, but some doctors get paid more in three months than some nurses get paid in a year. CEOs spend about the same amount of time at work as entry level employees, but CEOs typically make more in a month than entry level employees make in a year. Why is that you may ask? The answer is **value**. You do not get paid or get promotions based on time served/spent, you get paid based on your value. If your company pays you $10 an hour, it is because they think your value at work in an hour is worth $10. Otherwise, you can just stay at home, and they will send you a $10 check for every hour of your time.

I'll share two real life examples in my personal growth:

When I graduated with an undergraduate degree, I applied for a job in Memphis TN, the company offered me $40,000/ yr. because that's what they thought I was worth. I didn't get offended or angry. I was working as an assistant manager for Exxon gas station while I was going to school at the time. I quit my job and went to graduate school. I graduated with my master's degree and increased my value exponentially. In two years, my next job offer was way more respectable. Invest in your personal growth and development and then you can leverage your value.

In a different experience, I once asked my manager, a great young man with good character who I still have a great deal of respect for, if he had ever considered me for a promotion. He said "no". Because he did not believe that he had seen enough evidence in my work to consider me for a promotion. He went on to say that he believed I was doing a great job for the position I was in at the time but not good enough to consider me for a promotion. I appreciated his honesty, again, I wasn't offended or angry. But this time around it was different, so I reconsidered my stay at the company. If he had just said "if you want a promotion you will have to work on X, Y, and Z", I would have been more content with that. And the onus would have been on me to prove my value for a promotion. Instead, what his answer taught me was that the department or company did not value me enough to consider me for a promotion. Two weeks later, I submitted my resignation letter and to my surprise the head of the department invited me in for a one-on-one conversation and asked if I would consider staying if they offered me a promotion. I told him "No" because I was not looking for a promotion, I have never asked for a promotion at a job. I only wanted to know if I was valuable to my job and promotions and financial bonuses are usually the rewards used in Corporate America as a yardstick to measure an employee's value. I couldn't accept his offer because that was an indication that something was not right. Two weeks prior, my manager told me that he didn't see enough evidence in my work to consider me for a promotion.

And his superior was willing to offer me a promotion when I made my intention to walk away known to them.

This is a very common practice in Corporate America or in romantic relationships. People are sometimes conditioned by their employers or partners to believe/think that they cannot do better than their current situation or cannot do better elsewhere.

Around 1890 there was a Russian Physiologist and Psychologist called Ivan Pavlov, who did a study known as "classical conditioning" also known as "Pavlovian Conditioning", about salivation in dogs. He reported in his thesis that when he starves his dogs they begin to salivate whenever he walks into the lab. Because the dogs built a reflex stimulus response connection between his presence and food. The dogs automatically assume he is about to feed them anytime he walks in the room whether that is the case or not. This behavior is an unconditional response. Not to make a comparison between humans and dogs, but to say many people are suffering from "classical conditioning". You are conditioned by your partners, friends, relationships, employers, politicians, etc. to connect their presence in your life with satisfaction whether they brought you satisfaction or not. Whether they value or respect you or not. They mentally starve you of your needs and feed you when they see desperation in your eyes and can no longer say *no* to whatever they offer you. Liberate yourself from such conditional responses and relationships. For this reason, I turned down my director's offer to stay with the company and so I resigned.

A few days after I updated my LinkedIn profile, I received three job offers from senior managers at different companies for positions I never applied for. Even without a job application or interview, they already valued my services based on my resume and the work interactions I had with them previously. Your goal should not be to find a career that pays a lot of money. Find something you love doing and you are valuable at, and you will get paid a lot of money doing it.

In the first example, I was not valuable enough. I was not skilled enough. So, I went back to school and developed myself. In the second example, it was not that I lacked valuable skills, but I wasn't valuable to my team. I was probably a misfit, I don't know. LeBron James is the greatest basketball player today, but if you put him next to Leonel Messi, on the same F.C. Barcelona soccer team, he would be useless to them. But on the Lakers basketball team, he is an MVP caliber player.

Two things to learn here:

1. You don't get paid based on the time you've spent at work. You get paid based on how valuable you are at work.

2. Your value is also determined by your task and the team around you. In the right team, you can be an MVP. On the wrong team, you can be a liability.

4

Perseverance

— ✦ —

*"Perseverance is the hard work you do after you get
tired of doing the hard work you already did."*
- Newt Gingrich

The fourth step of Hustle Like an Immigrant mindset is perseverance. Ask any successful person you know, and they will tell you the endless hardships they've had to overcome in order to become successful. Like any other thing we live through, life will also test us. If you want to become a board certified medical doctor you must pass your residency, if you want to become a practicing lawyer you must pass the bar, if you want to become an accountant you must pass an accounting certification program (CPA), if you want to become a computer scientist/engineer you must pass your comprehensive exam, so on and so forth. Likewise, if you want to achieve your goals, you must pass the test of life. Life will test how resilient, tenacious, and committed you are. In order to become successful, you have to muster the courage to persevere through hardship. You can not allow excuses to prevent you from striving for excellence.

Whatever hardship you are going through, that same experience is a walk in the park for another person. Don't you ever get to a point where you start feeling sorry for yourself or succumb to victimhood. We have a saying in my Fraternity, Omega Psi Phi Fraternity Inc., that: *"excuses are monuments of nothingness that build bridges that lead to nowhere"*. When I first arrived in America, I was obsessed with attaining the goals I had set for myself and was relentless in pursuing them. On the days I didn't have enough food to eat - I fasted. The days I didn't have a car - I walked to work. The days my body ached, and I didn't feel well enough to go to work - I took medicine and toughed it out. The times I had bosses who didn't like me - I didn't care, I showed up on time to work every day with a good attitude. No matter what the obstacles were, I did not care or did not want to care, I was not going to be denied. This is the *Hustle like an Immigrant* mentality.

Here are the steps on how to develop a spirit of resilience and *perseverance*.

Learn to Deal with Disappointments:

In life there are some necessary losses. I'm not advocating for you to intentionally lose, but when you give your best effort and still lose, you must learn to master why you lost so that you can avoid failure the next time. Every day you wake up, look past your shortcomings, and look forward to what you could become. Let that be your motivation. Always aspire to be the best version of yourself and to never stop growing.

Life is a struggle, but you can choose your choice of struggle. Regardless of the choice, life is a struggle. Hard times are going to come and when they do, don't panic. It was Einstein who said, "we cannot solve problems at the same level of thinking that we were at when we created those problems". You must adjust/change your perspective when faced with challenges. Don't pray for easy times, pray for the strength and wisdom to deal with difficult or tough moments. Anybody can be faithful, positive, inspiring, loving, and calm during easy and good times. True character is best assessed during adversities.

What is your breaking point? Identify your breaking point, recognize it, embrace it, and persevere through it. Until you conquer your breaking point, you won't reach your greatest potential. Don't succumb to pain and quit. Don't allow fear to prevent you from advancing and progressing forward. And don't allow desperation to force you to renounce or compromise principles that are sacred to you.

> *"Success is not final; failure is not fatal:*
> *It is the courage to continue that counts."*
> **- Winston Churchill**

Success is not determined by what you have, it is determined by what you overcome. Don't take shortcuts, go through the process. Ask for help, if need be, but don't ask people for a free ride, ask for direction, and find your own way. You will be respected and better for it. If people take you everywhere, you won't learn how to walk on your own. Greatness comes out of struggle. Trust your struggle and have faith in your hustle.

Be Your Own Cheerleader and Ambassador:

I used to love weekends mainly because that's when I would watch F.C. Barcelona, my favorite soccer team, plays. I still love weekends but for a whole different reason. I'm a huge sports fanatic, well I was, I used to love sports. Soccer and basketball were life to me. I used to arrange my schedule around sporting games. And I used to spend a lot of my time watching my favorite sports teams and athletes work towards their dreams while I cheered and clapped for them like any loyal fan in the comfort of my living room couch. However, I used to dread Mondays when it was my turn to go to work and chase my dreams. I didn't have anyone cheering for me, I didn't even cheer for myself. Then I realized how foolish I was. I would cheer for my favorite athletes on weekends while they are chasing their dreams, but I would then dread going to work on Mondays to chase my own dreams. Be it Monday or Saturday, every morning when I wake up and get ready for work, I pretend like I'm wearing my very own jersey for a big game. And I cheer for myself like I'm about to take the last winning shot for my own team. Moral of the story, be your own cheerleader. Majority of the world wakes up every week looking forward to Friday. I dare you to be among the minority that wakes up every week looking forward to a productive 7-day week.

I have realized that we all often sell ourselves short. We are usually not comfortable talking about ourselves or what we do. We are either too timid or shy to market our own brand. But check this out: there is a Subway fast food restaurant at the corner of my residence. I know exactly where it is located, I know the menu like I know my name, and I even know the names of the employees there. But every day I turn on my TV there is a commercial about Subway as if I needed any extra motivation to keep going to their stores. Advertise yourself, market yourself, and be your own salesperson. You worked hard to get to where you are today without shortcuts, therefore why will you cut yourself short? Subway knows we know where they are located and what they sell, but that never stops them from advertising their products to us. Why then should you stop marketing yourself?

It's Never Too Late to Start:

A friend of mine once called to congratulate me on the publication of my inaugural book a few years ago. He told me how proud he was of me. He also expressed his disappointment in himself for dropping out of college and not completing his degree. I asked him why not go back to school and get his degree. He said it's too late for him, because by the time he goes back to school and gets his degree he will be about 40 years old. I told him that whether he goes back to school or not, he will be 40 in a few years. I told him I don't know about him, but I would rather be 40 years old with a degree than to be 40 years old without one. I have met far too many people who used this excuse of "it's too late". "I want to get back into my kids' life but it's too late now". "I want to call my family members I have not spoken to in years, but it is too late now". "I want to start my own business, but it is too late now". "I want to go back to school, but it is too late now". *It's too late* is the biggest excuse ever used to justify quitting or never starting. If you have life, then you have time to try again.

Become Immune to Being Told No:

The number one vitamin for success is being told "NO". If this word doesn't rejuvenate your desire for success, then you are not cut out for success. Rest if you must, there is nothing wrong with indulging in the finest thing life has to offer, with a healthy balance of course. But get back at it when you are rejuvenated like you have never been told "no" before.

Michael Jordan was dropped from his high school basketball team on his first tryout because the coach thought he wasn't good enough. Today he is a six-time NBA champion and arguably the greatest player to have ever played in the

NBA. Albert Einstein was not able to speak until he was four years old, and some of his teachers told him that he was a "retarded" kid who would never amount to anything. While I can't even begin to list all his accomplishments, I will highlight one: He received the Nobel Prize award in Physics for his services to theoretical physics, and especially for his discovery of the law of the photoelectric effect. Oprah Winfrey was demoted from her job as a news anchor because she was labeled too "fat and ugly" for TV. She is arguably the most influential woman in the world today and she owns her OWN TV station. At age 11, Lionel Messi was dropped from his youth soccer team because of growth hormone deficiency, he was too small they said. He is arguably the greatest soccer player ever and a seven-time FIFA world best player. At age 30, Steve Jobs was fired from the company, Apple, that he co-founded. A few years later, he got rehired. I don't think I need to tell you who Steve was, you are probably on your iPad, Mac computer, or iPhone as you read this. Almost all great people have failed at some point in their lives and have been told "no" or once rejected. If you have never failed in life, then you have never stepped outside of your comfort zone. We all had failures and shortcomings in our lives. We all have moments we wish we could do over. The wisdom is in never quitting or never giving up on your dreams.

What are your limits? Stop right there, you are limitless. If you can imagine it, you can attain it.

Soar on, I dare you to be great!

5

Risks

❖

"Everything is a risk. Not doing anything is a risk.
It's up to you."
- Nicola Yoon.

The fifth and final step of the *Hustle Like an Immigrant* mindset is taking risks.

You have to be willing to sacrifice who you are for what you can become!

Caterpillars are primed to become butterflies from birth. It takes a tremendous amount of perseverance for the caterpillar to become a butterfly. These insects typically live comfortable lives, they don't have many predators, their habitat is usually in heavily wooded areas and their diet primarily consists of the nutrients from wood. This is exactly why the metamorphosis of the caterpillar to a butterfly is quite extraordinary. This change isn't for the faint of heart because a butterfly isn't a caterpillar with wings, it becomes an entirely different being. Once the caterpillar makes this life changing choice, it first creates a chrysalis, a cocoon-like casing where it literally decomposes itself to usher in a rebirth. Then, it matures and develops in its cocoon until this space becomes too tight (a telltale sign for change) and at this point it breaks out of its once protective covering to soar through the air in all its newfound glory. The evolution of the caterpillar to a butterfly is very risky, painful, and dangerous, but it is a necessary risk to complete its life cycle. You too can embrace change like the caterpillar if you are willing to envision your end goal, stay committed to the process, and take calculated risks.

Like the caterpillar, everyone is primed to become successful from birth, but it is only those that work hard and take risks that become successful. Not everybody wants change, but for those who do, they must be willing to take calculated risks. These are the five steps of the risk-taking process:

Calculate and Evaluate the Risk:

You must conduct thorough analysis of the risk and the consequences of taking risk, and consequences of failure to take risk. You must answer questions like: is the reward or return on investment worth the risk? If unsuccessful, can the consequences be detrimental to my business or important relationships? Are there any safety concerns that could lead to loss of life or property? And so on.

There is a very thin line between taking a risk and being completely irresponsible. Making irresponsible decisions that puts oneself, ones' family, and business in danger when you can easily avoid it is not courage, it is basic stupidity. Therefore, one must weigh the pros and cons of every situation before taking any risk. Take small daily, weekly, monthly baby risks at a time, depending on the situation - to slowly build your confidence and risk-taking threshold.

Conquer Your Fears of Failure:

Many of us allow our innermost fears to become our most striking attributes. I have news for you, you will fail at something at some point, and you will be talked about. Be it in business, parenting, learning, family, performance, maiden expectations, etc. You will make mistakes. Be easy on yourself, learn to forgive yourself, learn to love and accept yourself wholeheartedly. Because the world will not forgive you for your mistakes. The world will judge you harshly for being different and audacious. The main wisdom is that: mistakes without lessons learned are just mistakes - mistakes with lessons learned are experiences. Know the difference.

If you ever fail at anything, make sure to fail your way to success. The reason I am able to enjoy and experience various levels of success is because I have learned how to benefit from the experiences of my failures. When I do something, I usually don't start from nothing, or from the bottom, I start from experience.

What if you try and fail? What if you don't make it? What if it becomes too hard and difficult for you? What if, what if, what if? What if Eve had never eaten the apple? The game of "what if" is a futile endeavor. My point is, I guess you will never know unless you have enough faith in yourself to try. What if you try and you make it? What if the only reason you are not successful is because you are scared to try? Just try it. Start using *I am/I will/I can* more often. Anytime you start a sentence with *I am/I will/I can*, the power of manifestation into the universe takes its effects and it is filled with endless possibilities.

One of the greatest entrepreneurs of our time, Jeff Bezos, was quoted as saying, "For me, I had to project myself forward to age 80. I don't want to be 80 years old, cataloging a bunch of major regrets of my life." By giving himself the benefit of the doubt and eliminating the dichotomy of "what ifs'", in 1994, Bezos risked it all by sacrificing his job in finance to found Amazon, which began as an online bookstore run out of his garage. Today, he is one of the wealthiest people in the world, with a net worth over $160 billion. Bezos' extraordinary story demonstrates how taking a leap of faith can lead to staggering successes.

I once worked at a place where the fear of losing our jobs was greater than our motivation to solve problems and to help the company grow. We went to work scared and left scared. Rumors of firings and force redundancies dominated our daily scrimmage. Even though many employees were miserable and hated their jobs, they wouldn't volunteer to accept a very lucrative six-month severance package that the company offered at the time. Many ended up being forcefully laid off later on with lesser severance packages to boot.

Let this sink in for a minute:

- For some of you, fear of a divorce and being judged is far greater than your love for your spouse.

- For some of you, the fear of failing at your dreams and life goals is stronger than your commitment to succeed.

- For some of you, your hate towards your fellow citizens motivated by your own insecurities and fears are far deeper than your love for yourself and your country.

- For some of you.... never-mind, you got my point.

Free yourself of fear and start living your life with a purpose. You must make a conscious and deliberate effort to make decisions based on your goals instead of your fears.

Embrace Change & New Possibilities and Ignore the Naysayers:

You must be willing, at any given time, to sacrifice who you are for what you can become. Progress rarely comes from those who are content and secure. It comes from those who are unsettled by what they have seen or experienced. Are you content and secured or are you unsettled by what you see? You will never be motivated enough to change what you can tolerate. Whatever is holding you back, I challenge you to be sick of it. When you can no longer accept something, you will change it.

The brilliant minds behind some of the world's most successful creations have one thing in common: they all embraced the positive possibilities of risk taking and betting on themselves.

To grow, you must be prepared to ignore people who hold stagnant opinions or views about you. You cannot change who you were in the past, you can only improve who you are now. You can only build on success. Don't fight against their limiting beliefs, whosoever they may be to you, stand up for yourself and if they take opposition to that then that's ok too. Don't say "no" to them, simply say "yes" to yourself and if that translates into a "no" for them then so be it. There is no need to prove them wrong, do it to prove yourself right, and if that by default proves them wrong then so be it. Do not be an anti to their beliefs, be pro to your personal beliefs and if that goes against their beliefs then so be it.

Change can come in different fashions. As you grow and mature, you will go through many changes. Growth without understanding and wisdom is not maturity, it is just aging. Your life is your story, if you don't like what you wrote yesterday, edit it to fit your current state or reality.

Sometimes people don't change, their feelings change. You are allowed to change your mind or position on issues when you know more than you previously did. This does not make one a hypocrite or a flip flopper.

Change is not new - the world has always gone through change of some sort and sometimes drastically. What has changed is the rate at which we experience change. The world is moving at an unbelievable speed, every day we wake up to almost a completely new world. You must be willing to adapt and be open to new experiences and opportunities.

Take Small Incremental Steps:

Not all risks have equal consequences. Some are more daring than others and require a more thoughtful approach. After conducting a thorough risk analysis, one may be advised to take baby steps. Take small daily, weekly, monthly baby steps at a time. Slowly build your confidence and risk-taking threshold. The first time you set out into a new endeavor, you may not want to put too much on the line. For instance, instead of quitting your career to pursue your entrepreneurship goals, maybe you can start by launching a part-time business or *hustle* and allow your career to finance your lifestyle as well as your small business, while you develop and grow your business to be self-sufficient. Once your business is up and running, and most importantly profitable, perhaps you will feel confident enough to make it your full-time job.

Seek Mentorship and Advice:

There is an adage; "you should learn from your mistakes". I said don't just learn from your mistakes, also learn from other people's mistakes. Because you can't make all the mistakes in this world by yourself. Whatever it is that you are going through, you are only experiencing what many before you have gone through. If the greatest athletes in the world all need coaches to coach them to play sports and identify their weaknesses and optimize their strengths, then you should equally have a coach or mentor to guide and help you manage risk in your life to achieve your goals and dreams.

Risk taking only applies to those who have the audacity to go beyond hard work and luck. Sometimes hard work alone is not enough. Everything involves risks. You must muster the courage to step outside of your comfort zone and challenge yourself.

If you take nothing else from this book, take this: the silliest phrase I ever heard in my life is "no new friends". Everything you need in this world you can get through new friends. Open your hearts and minds to new friendships and relationships. In fact, you should update and upgrade your friends list at least once every year. There are people somewhere who have the answers you are seeking. Keep seeking them out. Be relentless, never stop until one of them gives you the answers you are seeking.

Outro:

<hr>

"If you cannot do great things,
do small things in a great way"
-Napoleon Hill

We all know that we are supposed to wash our hands after using the bathroom or restroom, it is the most basic hygiene principle. But visit any public restroom and you will find a sticker/note reminding us to wash our hands. Let the *Hustle Like an Immigrant mindset* serve as a reminder for you to clean your act.

Ego and pride are not bad things. In fact, they are necessary ingredients for growth. Bad things are misguided ego and pride.

Francis Bacon said, "Knowledge is power", and Einstein said, "only if it is applied". I say, "knowledge is power when it is applied to benefit humanity". The prerequisite of success and growth is knowledge. You can't change your circumstances without the know-how. Your success will be incomplete until you become the answer to other peoples' prayers. Aspire to become other peoples' **amen**. Hope is a very fragile sentiment. The smallest thing can burst peoples' hope and the slightest error can also evaporate peoples' hope. Be kind with your words.

"You only get one shot, do not miss your chance to blow, because opportunity comes once in a lifetime..."
- Eminem

Youth is a blessing to the young in age, but like any other manufacturer, God limits its longevity with an expiration date as we age. Aging is a fact of life: we watch our parents, pets, and ourselves age along with non-living things like cars, clothes, and outdated electronics. Immortality is something we humans are not endowed with. Don't waste your youthfulness in foolishness.

There are about 78 organs in a human body, but the brain alone uses up to 20-25% of the energy in the human body. Your brain is the biggest consumer of your body energy. Don't waste it. Use it wisely.

Even God is disguised in discretion. Some things are meant to be discussed in private. Exercise some discretion with your personal life and avoid putting everything about you on public platforms.

Are You a Winner? The A,B,Cs of business says that "Always Be Closing". Winners don't just win - winners are also closers.

Are You a Leader? Leaders lead! Point blank period. There is no other way around it, leaders lead both in good times and not so good times.

Are You a Decision Maker? Be decisive. All good leaders are good decision makers. Muster the courage to be decisive. Thomas Jefferson once said, "in matters of style, swim with the current, in matters of principle, stand like a rock".

Finally, endeavor to travel the world and experience new cultures and learn new things. I can vividly remember during my freshman year in college in the U.S, I asked an American friend in a biology class if I could borrow her "rubber". She gave me the strangest look ever before replying "ask one of the guys". It took us five awkward and embarrassing minutes to come to an understanding that I was referring to a pencil eraser and not a... go figure. We both learned something new that day. Widen your horizon, learn about new cultures, expand your vocabulary, and be open minded. The world is bigger than your neighborhood or community.

Acknowledgement:

Firstly, I'd like to express my sincere gratitude to my supportive mother, Aja Sarata Ceesay. I am extremely grateful for her friendship and unconditional love. Special gratitude to my daughter, Asiya Kaddy Camara, and my son, Alieu Saikou Camara, for serving as my biggest inspiration. And my father, Mr. Alagie Alieu Camara who, even in death, continues to be my biggest motivating factor.

I would like to thank the following people who have helped me proofread, edit, and critique the book- multiple times. They have served as word editors, line editors, text editors, content screeners, and legal guides throughout the writing process. Justice Haddy Roche, Mr. Ebou Cham, and Jamal Drammeh, thank you for all the thoughtful comments and recommendations which were vital in inspiring me to think outside the box, from multiple perspectives to form and deliver a comprehensive and objective literature.

I would like to express my deep and sincere gratitude to Chelly Serge, CEO of IKOS Group and Remi Haget, Managing Director IKOS Group America, for their mentorship and support.

Finally, From the bottom of my heart I would like to say a big thank you to my readers who consistently invest in my publications and provide me with their feedback. Their reviews of my previous works have helped me improve on the quality and content of my writing.

Author's Biography:

Saikou is an international motivational speaker and a seasoned storyteller. As an African, storytelling is part of his culture, and it plays an instrumental part in his life. He perceives storytelling as an art form that links us to our past and gives us foresight into the future. He has been invited to speak at the White House, the United Nations, De Montfort University (Leicester City, UK), Bowie State University, Virginia Tech, RightsCon (Brussels), Portland University, University of the Gambia, Omaha YP Summit, among others. He is also the author of *Testimony of An African Immigrant – A Promise to My Father, Testimony of An African Immigrant II – Relentless Audacity,* and *Africa Through a Mirror – We have a Continent to Build.*

Saikou Camara is from The Gambia, West Africa. He traveled to the United States in 2004 to go to school. He graduated with his bachelor (BS) of Science in Computer Science from Rust College (2008), in Holly Springs Mississippi and graduated with his master's degree, in Computer Science, from Jackson State University (2010), in Jackson Mississippi. He now works as a Network Engineer/Project Manager/Consultant in the United States of America.

Saikou is the founder and the President of Your Change for a Change (YCFaC), a 501C3 non-profit organization incorporated in the state of Nebraska and registered in five different countries (USA, Gambia, UK, Sweden, and France). Saikou is currently serving as a board member for the Simple Foundation incorporated in Omaha Nebraska. As an activist with a passion for youth empowerment, Saikou co-founded the Global Leadership Empowerment and Diversity Summit (GLEADS) in 2016, which brings together a diverse group of young leaders to discuss innovative ideas and find solutions to our everyday challenges facing our diverse communities.

Saikou now draws from his experience as a trained IT professional and president for non-profit organizations to provide Project Development Consultancy for many start-up businesses and entrepreneurs especially in the field of technology and not-for-profit.

He was awarded the Superior Community Service award by the Black Employee Network (BEN) in 2014, and the Citizen of The Year award two years in a row, 2015-2016, by the Beta Upsilon Chapter of Omega Psi Phi Fraternity Incorporated. And in 2020, he was awarded by the Pan-African Youth Leadership as one of the 100 most influential young Africans of 2019 and 2020.